STILL HERE

Elin ap Hywel is a poet, translator and editor who works in Welsh and English. Formerly a translator for the National Museums and Galleries of Wales, Elin's published work has been widely anthologised and translated into Czech, English, German, Italian and Japanese. *Dal i Fod*, the original Welsh of *Still Here*, was shortlisted for Wales Book of the Year in 2021. Elin translated all of Menna Elfyn's dual-language texts, starting in 1995.

Laura Fisk is an NHS clinical psychologist, a poet and literary translator from Anglesey. Her poetry publications include *Coronavirus Chronicles - Коронавирус Хроники* (PNV Publications) translated into Macedonian by Julijana Velichkovska, and *Puid puudutada* (Allikaäärne) translated into Estonian by Ilmar Lehtpere. Both books deal with her experiences working on the coronavirus front line in 2020-21.

Also by Elin ap Hywel

Dal i Fod (Barddas, 2020)

Ffiniau / Borders (Gomer, 2002)

Pethau Brau (Y Lolfa, 1982)

CONTENTS

WHO WERE HELEDD'S SISTERS?	9
EMBROIDERY	11
BEFORE THE BLOOD COOLS	12
DIVINE PROVIDENCE OF HEAVEN	14
DAFFODILS	15
HYDRANGEAS	17
LYRIC	19
IDIOT	20
THE CREATURE	22
WISDOM	24
DAYS OF SERVITUDE	26
UNDER THE EARTH	29
SEPARATING	31
DREAM OF THE WELSHMAN	33
VAN GOGH'S LAST SELF-PORTRAIT	35
EAST WIND	37
END OF THE SONG	38
THE POEM'S A GAULOISE	39
AFTER	40
GODDESSES	41
GOLD	43
REPORT	45
FABLES	47
LAYING BARE	49
STITCHING	50
ONCE	51
THE VALUE OF FLESH	53
UNDERSTANDING ENLIGHTENMENT	54
IN MY MOTHER'S HOUSE	55
SEWING MACHINE	58
FEATHERS	60

IMBOLC	61
FLOWER	62
STILL LIFE	63
SNOW STORY	64
GO-BETWEEN	65
SONGS WITHOUT WORDS	67
CIRCLING	69
HALF MY SOUL	70
WORKHOUSE	72
THE HOME OF THE BARD	74
GALVANIC	76
BLUE	78
NAN	80
SLIPPING BY	82
SWEEPING	84
BEFORE THE NEXT WAVE	86
SOUP	87
USEFUL	89
POLITICAL CARTOONIST	91
UTTERANCES	93
HANDIWORK	94
BETWEEN TWO LIGHTS	95
WILLOW PATTERN, 1979	96
COWBOYS	98
CONSERVING	100
CANOPY	101
A COPPICE IN MIDDELHARNIS	102
SEARCHING	103
DEVELOPMENTS	105
SATING	108
ACKNOWLEDGEMENTS	111

 Cyfnewidfa Lên Cymru
Wales Literature Exchange

Published with the support of a Wales Literature Exchange Translation award through Arts Council of Wales National Lottery Funding

Published originally in Welsh by Cyhoeddiadau Barddas under the title of Dal i Fod. Welsh version copies available from https://www.barddas.cymru/

© 2025, Laura Fisk. All rights reserved. No part of this book may be reproduced, stored in a retrieval system, or transmitted in any form or by any means, whether electronic, mechanical, photocopying, recording, or otherwise, without the prior written permission of the publisher, except in the case of brief quotations used in reviews or scholarly works.

This work may not be used for text and data mining, including (without limitation) the training of artificial intelligence technologies or systems. The author and publisher expressly reserve all rights and opt out of any applicable text and data mining exceptions.

ISBN: 978-1-917617-35-2

Cover designed by Aaron Kent

Edited and Typeset by Aaron Kent

The author has asserted their right to be identified as the author of this Work in accordance with the Copyright, Designs and Patents Act 1988

Broken Sleep Books Ltd
PO BOX 102
Llandysul
SA44 9BG

Still Here

Elin ap Hywel
Translated by Laura Fisk

Broken Sleep Books

WHO WERE HELEDD'S SISTERS?

Imagine, if you will, the scene:
Pengwern, the colour of night. Heledd came
from the shadows and spoke
ribbonlengths of doleful old poems at the moon.

The whole thing's a lie: there's no quiet tonight,
normality denied. Everything
is as smooth as a lake in August, to the eye.
But one of two ears hears more than others:
Hush – in the quiet, the skeletons whisper.

It is only she that listens, listens and keeps listening
for she cannot look without seeing hands,
obliterated, on the picture. Tonight
there's a harmony in the chaos, peace
in the mute poetry of annihilation.

The hearth of gentleness extinguished.
What kind of place the pillars of community, custom and kin?
Tonight, it is madness that is primeval,
and it is tonight that chokes the memory, tight, like brambles.

It is only she that hears,

grey mice of doubts,

chewing at the quilt of old certainties,

and the weevils of wisdom

burrowing in the oaks of the past.

Contemplate the absurdity of her situation:

a prophetess perishing on the boundary,

quivering along the centuries between rhyme and reason,

a princess on the tide of remembrances. Nothing else,

a Cassandra of a Welshwoman without her rock in a man-less future.

Who were Heledd's sisters

plaiting patient purple of recollection

and the shade of suffering?

And how many Heledds

will wander the stillness of Wales's back history

and their shame clinging leech-like to their conscience

before striding beyond the border

that's more dangerous than the line on the map between

Welshperson and Englishperson?

EMBROIDERY

You wove into my hair

threads the colour of the rainbow,

and your fingers nimble,

illustrating

complexities of cunning love,

before tying the end of each plait

as tightly as the rituals of our romance.

But you're spinning lies now,

and the fine tundra of our forms

slackens,

labyrinthine lanes,

acts and articulations

uniting again,

the heart's pleats

unfastening

like the wattling of the days

when we were

one.

BEFORE THE BLOOD COOLS

Pencil marks

on a volume of cywyddau.

The graffiti of one mind

noting the excitement of the communion

with the thrill of the brine and the light burnishing white

on Dafydd ap Gwylim's seagull's feather,

on the unshakeable wall of time

twenty years and more ago –

"Vigour and youth rules, ok?"

Here is the spirit of the bard

who's eager to drag the bright paint of his experiences

across live bricks,

and painting the world

in green

and red

and yellow

and orange

and blue, –

having commemorated it forever

in surprised scribbles of grey graffiti;

a bard who revered

and who today pushes

arcs of the electricity that lightnings in a rainbow of poem

through tight wires of their nostalgia.

Oh, come to me the wisdom

to live the ardour of my song

in the short minute

before the spectrum of life

turns to black and white,

and before my pain turns

into a volume of observations

that slowly lose their colour

on the edges of the brittle pages of my memory.

DIVINE PROVIDENCE OF HEAVEN

I was shepherding my precious bestowment

From day to day; one in a flock of show sheep,

Each one folded safe, once come its moment

Into the sheltered pen of memory, with that, a leap

Along the wide valley of abundant vows,

Trampling the earth, destroying the white plantations,

And preventing, through plundering the plough's

Potential yellow harvest of these aspirations.

But one escaped towards the mountain-ledge

Along uncertain steep paths, the moon illuminating

My swirling fear, pressing heavy on the edge

Of a no-turning-back precipice of cold lunacy

Unreliable is the world, while the wolf of tomorrow stalks,

Hidden, poised to beguile the lambs of the flocks.

DAFFODILS

Touching them is an almost carnal act

stealing to memory

the flash of the edge of the blade of sunlight

striking the hay, and the echo

of dogs baying between the walls of the barn of the mind.

The moist and smooth yellowness of the petals lies

like skin between the fingers

its sap throbbing green

in the veins,

co-mingling in the veins

appearing as rust on a sword, like heather on a cliff.

Through the eye of the stamen, the microscope of the past

brings back into focus all our passionate minutes

in scintillas

close to the trembling mist of morning

and again, far,

so far from the moment

that Llywelyn was killed,

and his soul slipped into the darkblackness

like a droplet falling from a leaf.

All of the whole is in it – reach your hand and touch it –

the short-lived life

that dares for a while

and then withers to the soil. Press it

between the damp pages of your heavy responsibilities,

in an emblem of a seasonless spring

in the hazy teeth of autumn. The flowers still

dance mute-blindly, puppets of the wind.

HYDRANGEAS

The pink ultra-pink, the blue a calcification of blue

that scratches the afternoon like chalk on a blackboard of yesteryear

the way that they grow

in boiling hot gardens, a municipality in the sun.

Their toilet-paper colours.

The leaves, like palms fat in their width that say

"I've nursed roots by now".

Even the white ones – too white, somehow,

not the flimsy whiteness of Japanese paper

but the whiteness of a nothing-nothing, an absent whiteness,

negative, empty, too bloody-bloody boring.

A sign of being middle aged is liking hydrangeas,

discussing the way the soil will

colour some blue, the others pink,

conferring on how to fool nature

through shovelling lime on top of acidic soil.

Doting then on the way

each flower is a smaller flower, a star that nestles

inside a bigger star; perfect, round, worlds,

infatuated with their beauty in their decline,

a sober rainbow

the brown, the grey, the yellow, glorying in their hydrangeas.

LYRIC

If I would give to you the secrets of my body,

my breasts white against the blackness of night

and receive them into the recesses of my flesh,

and grant me freedom?

Freedom from feeling the weight of your fingers

tracing the shape of some love that's got lost

on the clay of my skin, and freedom

from tasting the platitudes you sow

around me, as if they were green and soily

freedom

from knowing

that I am only a twig on the path through the forest is what I am.

If I were to give you my entirety, would you,

look at me once, without

pretence, and say, "I love you"?

IDIOT

You're laughing like the god Pan,

your face a sky of feeling,

puffs of your capriciousness

sending charges

in clouds to dart across the horizon of your eyes.

Every morning,

you are there on the street corner,

like a song thrush

watching the snails

that trek towards the concrete forest

through the long blades

enclosing the light above their heads,

and a thousand windows of the flats shimmering

like the sun as it strikes the dew

on the morning pasture.

Yours,

the street and its fullness –

the cry of children,

resounds

through the wooded patches of your mind,

and the agitation of the traffic

explodes in a thrill of greenness

in one of the fruitful corners

of your imagination, that comprises

the world and resides there.

While I watch you

like a cat

between stiff parlour curtains

that rustle between my fingers

with the whisper of withered leaves –

watching you,

watching those who slink by,

the secrets of the big world

that are to be had in the dark heart of the forest,

leaving behind them a slippery trail

to shine like

silver

in the empty streets.

On the road to work

I tread carefully

to avoid trampling

the traces of the pyramids

on the dust of the dry pavement.

THE CREATURE

Too late.

You crucified your prey

on the keen spears of your sights.

Waiting.

Watching.

The rhythm of the teeth grazing the hay

plucking the string in your memory,

the drums of death

thumping in your ears,

increasing with the wild song of your blood

establishing the tempo of the dance.

So tender

the smooth swelling of the skin swells the memory.

Remembering the steps is easy,

as easy as sinking jaws around meat,

as comfortable as the slackening of swaddling,

ready for the leap.

Your partner is a virgin in the intercourse with death
but she knows the etiquette of the dance.

Its slow swaying, on legs
as slender as the dry rushes of the meadow,
as the jingle of a feast of bones,
and the dread that flows to his eyes,
clouds your memory with the blood
rising like wine to intoxicate
the discretion of your senses.

The last bosom friend is ecstasy,
and death caresses his body.

And in the silence
we hear the sound
of distant pipes calling the beginning of the feast.

WISDOM

You speak

in concrete, no-nonsense,

your forty years' experience -

there's an artificial sheen

to the silver paper of a child's present

to the mist, rising from the magic castles

that I saw on the horizon over there.

You narrated

in that the critical way of yours

towards a similar castle

in the small hours of the morning.

A pack of hopes lay

in soft smoothness on your shoulders,

and you with a sickle with its edge of brilliant ambition,

reaping the path

through the intricate brushwood

to snatch your prize

and capture the castle.

You crept

towards the promise

that swirls in a column of cloud the colour of daylight,

that sparkles in a column of fire the colour of night,

by following the leaves

in the melody of some shapeless soul,

without noticing the ideals falling like leaves around you,

nor listening to a farewell song for every chance lost.

The harsh echo,

the melody a mockery,

from the corners of your empty fort,

and you now are the speaking clown

flouting effort

by the embers of the dying fire.

DAYS OF SERVITUDE
to some of my contemporaries, 1977-1980

Days of servitude were these.

The whole world was there

in the streets of the town,

and days of walking

through labyrinthine grey streets

a constant background

to the transparent flash

of the film of imagination

while each step

compels us towards nothing.

In the drunkenness

of a lazy August afternoon,

the laziness enticing us

from the open tavern doors of the High Street,

and the comfortable sourness

of the years of joyful evenings

 is dust on the ground.

Through the wild mustiness of the afternoon

we created

the iron bars of our prison

from the molten metal

of lifeless stories of the unemployed,

our pool Odyssey without roots in the soil,

recollections

of splendid days

that lost their blazing brightness

seasons ago.

Then, venturing to twilight

and the hot breeze

combing the dust

to the secret corners

of the darkness.

The dark days of the experimental kiss,

restrained by fear of mind and flesh,

while the lip searches new ways to love.

We breed

the keeper of our gaol

of romantic words.

Eggshell of love

hiding the nut of desire,

law of the tribe

proclaimed to us a surfeit

for imagining that this is what was real.

Turn the corner to see

the Serengeti of the future

a menace before us.

Wilderness,

where come the vultures of paranoia

to feast on uncertainty's mincemeat,

where it's easy

to fall prey

to the lion

of possibilities.

The freedom of our tomorrow's devastation

was the greatest

restriction of all.

UNDER THE EARTH

As the mouth of the tunnel sucked in the train

and swallowed it down the narrow throat of its blackness,

I knew that I had lifted a ticket

at the station whose name I didn't know.

I had stepped unthinking onto the train

along with a swarm of other travellers,

and feeling the exciting force of the machine

driving the cars in a whirlwind of dust

to rush past

the stunned faces

it leaves alone on the platform

to raise their hands

in a flaccid gesture, in a half-farewell.

From one to another

I left my fellow-travellers;

stepping purposefully

towards work

at age

at life

through the electric doors

that would always slam shut

before I decided

that I wanted to follow.

I'm permitted here

to watch the adverts on the walls

radiating past

in an innovative slash –

Barbados –

heavens on Earth,

a glance

at the distant paradise

before the train

speeds toward the tunnel,

the insane grin of the porter by the gate

in my salutation as I arrived at the end in a cloud of ash.

SEPARATING

I am an island

one stone

in the middle of a sea of bodies

sinking and floating

in each other's arms

and me watching them,

one stone

far

incredible.

You came to me

To embrace me like a wave

entice me

into the wild race

and foam of excitement,

throw me to the water

that spurts and leaps.

We coalesced

creating a flash between two stones

electricity

like amber

In the tenderness of the sea around us

light

stupefied along the edges of the shores.

With that,

you left.

You went

like the tide slipping on the ebb

from off the naked rock

by furthering

slowly

towards the horizon,

nothing

but another wave

falling to oblivion

in a sea of waves.

Without the spark

we are nothing at all

but idle stones watching the water's dance.

DREAM OF THE WELSHMAN

Last night you went to him,

so promising as a ripe damson,

and your warm skin tickling his senses,

your arms

a mother's arms

and her child sucking milk from her breasts,

and your cruel tenderness

tugging at the covenant without completion –

at the secret of language

that waits between the warmth of your loins –

the key to the door on Aber Henfelen his regrets,

land echoing the call for lost love.

Today, he wakes to the mixed-up listlessness of the sheets,

to the dirty dishes and mood of last night

clinging like old yolk to every plate;

waking

to the day that's putrefaction before it's begun,

and its wet fog that's lifted from the corpse of his dreams;

waking

to a day so unenchanted

as flat beer at the bottom of his glass.

You betrayed him.

enchantress for one night, you were,

despite you promising wifely faithfulness; and this,

who'd be so foolish

as to comb suspicions last night

into a pile, to sweep them

like dust under the carpet of night.

Today he counts his hopes

the ash of the cigarettes he smoked,

needing them for your treacherous kiss

an appetite that will stir up

and embitter

his nightmare tonight.

VAN GOGH'S LAST SELF-PORTRAIT

Picture: a crossword of makeup

an old Welsh poem on canvas of the past,

a mirror to the future

to remember the essence

of what I was.

Oh yes, I got days of my madness

days of sun-scorched Provence

a fire on my skin, mornings' dew

tears on the cherry tree's cheek

that stretches out its fragile fists towards the azure,

the late sun

setting like a snail across the wheat fields,

and nights of indigo

and the wretches of the city

whisper from each street.

I was a sorcerer of faces,

I was a wizard of images,

I was an artist.

And the whole thing comes back to this –

the magic that twinkles from the sky on an August night

in the round hollows of the pools of my eyes,

a rainbow of humanity that I saw

a lock in the casket of the skull

and the golden force

that shines from the background of yellow corn

so weak

as the gleanings of a ginger beard

that cling to my chin.

I'm broken in.

and in the fakery of days to come I will be so;

the fox that grew wise,

the flame that became established,

without a sign

for you that came from the woe I saw,

except for the pangs of paint in the background

that meander forever

towards – what?

EAST WIND

East Wind – tearful this evening

whispering a sacrament

through the skeletons of trees.

East wind – a muse this evening

its melody an elegy

above the graves of freshly fallen leaves.

East wind – spits this evening

its lash of contempt

on the backs of blackened leaves.

East wind – crying this evening

its tears soft hypocrisy

funeralising for things living.

East wind – calm will come tomorrow

and the storm sinks

into the blood of the west.

END OF THE SONG

The red lights go off –
the song dies on the lips of the radio
and the button chokes the sound of the blues.

Only whispers are left.

That's everything that's wanted
to abort all sugar sentiment of the words
that promise that romance will last forever,
will leave us here
in the pregnant silence
and only the echo of the chorus
a lullaby
to our stillborn chat.

"All you need is love".

Then, listen
the form of the melody in our feeling
quietens discordantly,
somewhere where there's a radio
still declaring
that love is the answer.

THE POEM'S A GAULOISE

The poem's a Gauloise –

a stump for us to suck the nicotine of imagination;

smouldering

between the mind's fingers,

by freeing emotions

like a ribbon of blue smoke

turning in the spacious hall of Memory;

before it expires

and is tossed

to the waste paper bin,

to the dusty subconscious.

AFTER

The doctor came –

put the ring

in the man's hand.

She lay there

her life

a sparkling circle

in the palm of her hand.

GODDESSES

Goddesses of Wales,
goddesses of the broom, the oak, meadowsweet blossoms,
the dry bones, claws in the fur,

it wasn't you who was treading through my dreams
years ago in my school-girl bed,

but feeble minor-goddesses, whose comings and goings are but
fickle flourishes between Greek and Roman myths
a rainbow for a second, and there in a river or a shrub,
always between two thoughts and two forms,
pleasing some man, hiding in case of some god,
changing their names and themselves like changing lipstick:
Echo, Eos, Psyche – sixth-form girls
laughing behind their newly-washed fringes.

Come to understand your ways, I did -
slowly, reluctant, dour like drowning cats,
with every bruise I saw, every empty kiss,
every ring in the palm of a hand, came to understand anger –
scenting the blood on the hands and the iron house warmth,
hearing the skulls of children clunking in the wind.

Queens of the wild, the crazy, the people out of their trees,
the un-warm quietness, the great uneasiness -
you keep company tonight in the lament of the news,
stalking through the room in your tattered satin gowns.
the tiredness of the years is a wound beneath your eyes
and your skin is crinkly apples;

but the lightning and thunder are electricity in the cloud of your hair,
the apron of some giantess a girdle round your bellies,
and the clover of your white fury is tight around your heels.

Islands of mighty men upset at the fringes of your petticoats.

GOLD

When I was a girl, I heard told
beneath our family fields lay gold

the bones of a woman there, covert,
in a dark bed under the dirt,

and plain truth that the ploughshare's trail
left behind drops of gold at such scale

so fine as the leftovers in the wood shed
or the cloud of hair upon my head.

He expressed reproach, and in our feed
scolded me over the mead

and he reproached again when I came back
from the market, a whole full sack

pressing wounds across limbs
until my life was a shiver of stings,

but the gold sang out, unfurled,
in a grave under a hill at the end of the world

and that's how our life nearly went
listening on to its old circular lament.

***

The esteemed gentleman came this way
and planted spades in the hay

and said that the grave was full of gold,
shining as bright as the sun to behold

and that all the little mousey pests
were plaiting gold to line their nests,

and tonight my hair is white.
To myself, a story I will write –

about the life of the queen getting
ready for the blood wedding,

red silk all rags and tatters
skin rotting back to the earth in shatters

and nothing left before our eyes
but mud and gold where she lies.

REPORT
from the "Rhiannon" series

By now, I'm proud to say,

everything is starting to come together;

I'm starting to become accustomed

to ornithology.

(I feel now, since a century or two,

that flying comes more easily. The balance

between the right wing and the left has improved

and the process of landing is much smoother.

Aerodynamic. That's the word.)

It's a big step, looking back.

Sometimes, the past will

squeeze nastily on my stomach,

a heavy bullet that's full of bone and fur,

Especially on the evenings of summer –

and that second, between evening dusk and morning twilight

while the world is a rush of a flourish of wings,

and a life as short as a mouse's memory,

a tiny squeak between two darknesses.

But at that time I could remember:

I didn't like the way

the multicoloured silk gowns

clung to my flank in the heat

and those everlasting afternoons

when Llew placed his hand on my thigh.

Yes we are, feathers are much better,

dry and smooth, like leaves or flowers.

They don't show the blood.

They're much easier to keep clean.

FABLES
from the "Rhiannon" series

I remember one better than the rest.

A cook, she was.
She held her fattened haunches around my middle
as if they were trying to knead
my mouth empty of the spew of the days,

but as her mottled heels
struck bruises on my bosom
portions of history extended
until my barren lips
slavered for the want of knowing more –

histories of foster mothers as wolves,
of strange love, children that went missing,
fables about fishermen and shepherds
giving lodging to angels without knowing –

a story about a king of one of the dark lands
who left a child, in his nappies, in the snow
a sovereign in his mouth. His fingers seized
in a knot in my mane while reporting how
he was raised by bears.

One evening

the bear and its children slinked back to the palace.

Spat out the sovereign into its father's mead cup.

The bears tore their grandfather into living lumps.

I left her topsy turvy by the port,

talking of swans, peacocks, pies, wines.

Her last words crossing the threshold:

'They will eat the king, with cloves and rosemary'.

LAYING BARE
from the "Rhiannon" series

Taking off his armour was the greatest ceremony.

The steel pieces shone with resonance,

scale by scale, to the floor.

I divested him of

family, tribe, neighbourhood, kinsman, and country.

Scab by scab, I removed

layers of his history from him

along the last coat of mail, where

my hand lay in the space between metal and flesh.

STITCHING
from the "Rhiannon" series

As the edges of the frame frayed, I remember

a day of white and yellow, air and gold.

Dale, flowers, birds. The pasture is green plush velvet.

Some hand stitched the horse and me into the picture.

Sensed the needle piercing through me.

Embroidered the last curl in the war-horse's tail

and left there, in a weaving of sparkling threads.

A century passed. Hooves heard behind,

and then, it cried.

The moment split

like a sword glistening through silk.

The stitches loosened, I walked

out of the design, straight to the eye of the sun.

ONCE

Once

in a distant land

in the Dark Ages,

there was a king

– a queen, too -

descended from a tribe of deer,

her from the tribe of the mares and goats.

Her body was white

like a long streak of milk,

itself so stout as an antler.

They married at seven years old,

living half a century together, and raised

twenty children;

she sat in her chamber sewing,

he thundered in the big forest

and though they didn't love each other,

it was his hair she saw as she spun the wool,

her skin he saw as he drew the arrow,

from the flank of the doe he'd killed -

In the end,

as the gold and bronze and the wine the colour of blood

and the silk, and the ambassador

from the land where the ginger and indigo grows,

the king and the queen did die

their hide a long tome of years –

they were buried

in the same grave –

her in the leather mantle of the mare,

him, according to the ritual of the tribe of deer,

with antlers on his head:

the type as tough as steel;

and the rain fell on their grave.

THE VALUE OF FLESH

The value of ox hide, its tough might: eight pence.

The value of stag hide: eight pence.

The value of cow hide, lactating, creamy: seven pence.

The value of doe hide: seven pence.

The hide of sheep, and goat, roe-deer [male or female]: a penny each.

The value of fox hide: eight pence.

The value of otter hide, his wisdom concerning

the depths of the river: eight pence.

The value of wolf hide: eight pence.

The value of sable hide, the fine glittering fur: twenty-four pennies.

The work of the king's gatekeeper: the preparation of hides

of creatures killed on the palace floor.

Payment for this: a penny the hide.

For the shame of the king's gatekeeper: six cows,

one hundred and twenty shiny silver pennies.

Their eyes, their open mouths, their teeth, their claws.

UNDERSTANDING ENLIGHTENMENT
In memory of the artist Gwen John

Sometimes, on Sunday afternoons, and the light is cold,

she sees her face for what it is –

the sun etching the bones of her cheeks,

and the circles of the years under her eyes.

At the top of the morning, at the offering

– while the rest are at their prayers in a world that's full of light –

she marvels at the folds

in the wimple of the nun in front of her.

How can white linen be the same colour as dust?

Last night, by the radiance of the lamp, she left

a loaf of bread and knife on the table,

and before eating, lifted her pencil.

Tonight, she'll finish her sketch,

drawing the cat on the rocking chair.

she knows the girl's hair that bends towards the light

is the same colour as a droplet of blood that's slow to dry.

IN MY MOTHER'S HOUSE

In my mum's house there are many residences,

parlours that are a dance of air and light –

the tea crockery on the tablecloth already

and the curtains open to display the view

of the sea, without one ship. Corridors,

brown, and dark, that wind for miles

and miles to somewhere, before ending, abruptly

in a scullery where the dishes whisper on the shelves,

and the pipes groan and rasp moodily.

Stairs that wind down and down and down

past pictures of the family on the flock walls –

look there's Nain! There's a stoat around her neck! –

as they reached that bad place,

the cellar full of burned bones,

skulls of children, like the shells of eggs.

Tonight, I forage for the bathroom,

a tiny Antarctic of glass and marble.

I've been here before, to play with the soap,

shooting it through my fingers

in order to leave a slippery

snail's path of tears, by thinking ever so quietly:

if I should succeed in putting my head under the tap
the drip-dripping will improve my sickness.

I've come to this house every night since the funeral,
have walked and danced and crept through places
and their geography changing on the wind's wing.
I dote on the back kitchen, on the dresser
that's a solid hunk of black oak,
more similar to a loaf of bread than a piece of furniture,
and the name of my uncle chiselled into its side.
The Staffordshire china dogs
stand like soldiers above the glass plates,
their sloe eyes of jealousy.
Sometimes, if I'm lucky, they'll chat with me:
she's newly left. She's in the corridor.
You've just missed her, you have! –
and I'll catch a glimpse of her skirt hem.

One time, I'll never forget, I went to the parlour,
and she was there, sitting there in a chair before the fire.
She extended her hand, small hand, the hand of a harpist,
the fingers long, fine and white.
I folded my fingers into her fingers.
Not a word was spoken. Complete embarrassment

of us being caught communing on the other side of the veil.

Today I don't know how I left the room.

I'm searching for her each time I go back.

Sometimes, the room is there, sometimes it's not.

Sometimes, her cup and saucer are on the table.

Sometimes, the fire is embers, cold, grey.

SEWING MACHINE

A table of wood

that opens out

like a conjuror's table

its drawers full of mysteries

about grandma who died before my birth,

leaving the little cupboards closed like a tree who's buried its seeds.

I would move the telly sometimes,

open the lock, finger the spaces

where thrifted reels of cotton and silk,

the patterns, the pin papers

– as if I were looking for something

that lost night, maybe –

that plays on the television of my imagination

in the back parlour of the coal village

when the Singer steamed as a polished engine,

the plate singing under her foot,

glowing cinders warming her in the compulsion of the machine

to push, dart, and crimp

to tailor the cloth of her love

into everyday things – shirts and pants

(the winter necessities of two kids)

before the stitches fail to come together.

Yes,

that night

the radio playing Family Favourites,

the material obedient and smooth under her hand,

the wheel gleams, the line sure and tight.

FEATHERS

So difficult it is to weigh and measure feathers.
To put forth your fingertip to touch them,
reform them through your hands,
one breath is what's in them.
 You may not amass them;
a second or two whirling
then disappearing on the wind's tongue
to snowdrift on the palate on some overbridge.

They tremble there
on the edge of the night,
so quiet, so accusingly,
and with the soaring dawn
from one to another, mottling with apostrophes
through the grey sky. Above the roadways and old fields
they swarm nimbly,
the whispering of their quills an earnest murmur
to speak aloud as they explode
into a sparkling shower along the streets

and to lie, for their whiteness,
so substantial in their plenty
so undeniably substantive
as steel, as concrete, as coal.

IMBOLC
festival of Saint Brigid that marks the beginning of spring

She's the one

who knocks the door

between sleep and waking,

a warm milking cow

who stretches the sun to warm you,

pouring a milk-gift into your teacup.

Through the night, you were dreaming

of the bonfire and its long tongue flames

of cotton, of silk, of blood.

No answer.

She rests the bottle

with a clatter on the threshold.

Between last night and today,

hear her carriages bellowing along the street

on an electric ram.

In the kitchen the blue milk's

a shiver of ice on your tongue.

FLOWER

An idle one, Sharon is. A spiky, brittle one,

who's folded in on herself;

an unyielding husk, brown

like bark

the last chestnut tree of autumn.

Some say that her smile is pleasant

though rare – in truth, it's more pleasant

for being as water in the desert,

but the truth about it is

that no one's seen her proper petals

since a year or two.

But give her a drop

on the right day, in the month of the extreme weather -

a teardrop, or gin, or thunderous rain,

and she'll explode into a cupful of dewy rose

who turns her even face towards the flow

and soaks it bravely from the eye of the storm.

STILL LIFE

Crimson saffron

its tongue as yellow as the centre of an Easter egg;

the light of the north

a shiver of ice

on the tough enamel mug.

You are my image of Holland:

the small fissure that lets loose light,

by turning every thing

strange familiar.

SNOW STORY

The big guns crackled for the last time
and quiet descended upon the fields, on the trees, on the sea –
dropped from the air slowly, like snowflakes,
cold and strange, to sear on children's tongues.
What kind of thing was their peace? Bananas a shilling and sixpence,
nylon stockings, Nain dancing? I don't much believe it.
An acute breeze whipping their cheeks aflame later,
footprints of hobnailed boots in the white wilderness,
hands grasping the wet strangeness to fold it
into snow balls and boulders, trampling the fine powder.
And when the stars came to prick the conscience of their day
and the moon to illuminate the dark corners of the night,
we ran along the road towards the kettle and the fire,
far, far away from the playing fields and their laughter.
The rain dropped like bullets on the marsh, on the mire,
and on the vast plains.
There was nothing left of the miracle
but dirty pools and the odd wet pocket handkerchief.

What kind of thing is our peace? Bananas in every shop,
silk stockings, everyone dancing? I don't much believe it.
Sitting and watching the snow thawing, later,
and turning from the window, back towards the kettle and the fire.

GO-BETWEEN

Darling, I send a love-message to you –
a sweet-nothing straight to the heart,
illiterate interpreter of my feelings
itself full of wordless eloquence.

But there are so many things in the world;
which one will be the best choice?
The one that précises all the yearning
the exact thing?

Seagull?

Mare?

Stag?

– Or a flower, maybe?
White hawthorn, or a rose, or cactus –
something a little spiky
that's on the verge of flowering all the same.

No.

I will send a handbag to you:

a knapsack filled with stupefaction

that's a wilderness of mercies.

I wrap my letter in skin.

Its contents:

a serviette, and ideas about a poem,

a very strong mint (in case a kiss will come),

a plaster (in case of a tumble).

Phone numbers of anonymous people,

a sock, and its silky armour

strong and slippery between the fingers.

A knife, and in it a weapon against any thing

except the key that opens secrets.

In the pocket, five pounds and pesetas from Spain.

In the pocket and zip, who knew?

In the bottom one, nothing but hair and dust.

Darling, I will send this to you

– a sack that's full of incomparable flux

that will speak its knowledge of me

– and the burden of its gossip will be:

make a woman of these things!

SONGS WITHOUT WORDS

I know a boy who listens to songs without words
each evening in his blue bedroom,
he hears castles collapsing, and cities sinking
between the piano and the bass guitar.

I know a girl who watches old films,
closing the curtains and turns off the picture,
she wants to put herself
in the place of Bette Davis and Lauren Bacall
and in place of black and white, sees the screen
all in kisses.

I know a boy who lives on the moon,
he flies through space each night
and the dust of Ursa Major living silver in his hair
when he arrives back from his wandering;
he thinks he's a giant
a hero come to rescue the world.

I know a man who climbs the stairs
once he's turned off the gas,
who listens to the radio – the World Service –

listening to the story of his mum and dad

between the news bulletin and national anthem,

a man who knows yearning like snow

warm and cold, all over love,

a man who rises the next morning to open the curtains

to see there's ice on the street.

CIRCLING

One day Big Ben lost five minutes when
a flock of starlings perched on the big hand of the clock.

If the starlings who swirl
in a soaring maelstrom above the prom,
in circles that continually tighten,

were a churn that stirs up our minutes,
what would happen to our days?

What if the beating of the wings,
the singlemindedness of the birds and their purpose, an incantation

that would give us the five little minutes
that are so scarce in our lives,
the five minutes that we always promise
to our lovers, and our grans, and our children –

and what if those minutes turn into dreams about flying,
a feathered comfort of belonging,
a power of knowing our purpose
dawdling towards some aim?

HALF MY SOUL
Winnie Mandela

half a heart

half a beat

half a wife

half a lover

half a mother

half a child

half a female

half a handmaid

half a song

half a note

half a prayer

half a hymn

half an anthem

half a lament

half a hell

is my purgatory

half rising

half life

half falling

penance, penance

half promising

half believing

half asking

half imploring

half dead

half murdered

half communion

half baptism

half dark

and half treachery

a whole folk

less than a country.

WORKHOUSE

'It's similar to a shell

– to an eggshell

– to a ping pong ball

– to a plastic cup out of a coffee machine

– to a letter from a relation that you haven't seen for ages'.

Here we are, tremblers, extending a whole fistful of breath

from hand to hand. Behind closed eyes

the thought that's between us is large like an iceflow,

our fingers scrambling to join, somehow,

born of this strangeness

before turning, and spilling it into the crucible of the next hands –

myself like a wolf peering through my fingers

to see the children's faces, their astonished eyes,

and this idea that moves through the quietness

like a great feather that strikes a sea of light,

and to see

that they understand, now,

that a buzzard skull is what this husk is, that's like

a host of things, dark and light –

a snail's shell that's spiked with breastwork

the hollow in a field that holds the ice and keeps it;

a beating of darkness that awaits a candle;

a small present I fear to open,

an envelope of bones without a stamp, without address.

THE HOME OF THE BARD

This is a house that pulls light,
that unfolds its white energy
in sheets of sun that lie
along the stairs and the floor.

It minces air, throws sparkliness
in a messy blanket over the sofa and the stove,
throwing it in bright ribbons that strike
the tiles and the taps in the shower
before making its den on the floor of the porch.

In the study, the whole is dark
– the blinds having slammed their mouths shut
against the town's chattered Saturday night stories;
the ideas of philosophers and proud poets of the world
sleep between cardboard covers
to old hymns, plump on the piano.

And on the desk, a scrap of paper
that's smaller than a child's hanky
soft, dumb, wordless,
waiting.

In its folds is the world.

It lies there. It waits for blood.

GALVANIC

Neither one of the two –

neither the technophobic minister

nor his agnostic daughter –

despite his physics lessons,

understands the microwave.

They don't understand where the warmth comes from.

'It's similar to faith', says the girl –

'It's soundless,

odourless,

colourless,

and yet, somehow, it changes things'.

And it's true.

There's some unseen force

playing hide-and-seek with the molecules

until the transubstantiation of the fish and loaves,

is a code in hot, crunchy crumbs.

The trouble is, there are so many rules.

One must pierce the skin of thick-skinned things,

one must protect the skin of thin-skinned things,

but NOT with foil, or otherwise

The whole will explode or blow its fuse.

The two stand on the threshold of Christmas

staring not-understanding at the miracle.

This is her dream: some night

she comes home late. In the kitchen

the only light comes from the belly of the oven

where the baked potato pirouettes through the chasm,

waiting for the final, certain, ping.

On each plate, on the table, on the counter,

on top of the breadbin, on the fridge, on the floor,

her father catered the feast –

a pudding jewelled with currants and cherries,

flooded in custard,

a Titanic of a turkey,

an Eden-ful of green vegetables.

Under the penetrating eyes of white energy

she pulls up her chair and starts to commune.

BLUE
in memory of Derek Jarman

A tortoise of a man on the box. His skin

is primeval, anciently old, as if

some hot wind had tormented it into a husk

rind without juice and without scent.

Tortoise of a man without a shell who's jerking

his head unstably towards the camera

seeing if the world is still there.

I have so much of a desire to touch him -

to reach, somehow, into the telly,

and harrow the basins under his eyes with my thumb,

to place a fingertip on the parchment of his cheek

and to say one 'thank you' quietly

– for the civility of satin, for shine,

for powder and paint, for pain,

for rivets, for candlelight,

for grapes, for strawberries, for wine,

for velvet, for the warmth of breath,

for excess, for exultation. For gilding

the black and white of the screen and the rainbow of

the colours slipped from one to one

and only blue is left now, blue

that's a true blue, like the sky or the sea,

the smoke that whirls from the first fag of the morning,

petrol on the road after a shower of rain,

the little bag of salt at the bottom of a bag of crisps –

but blue that's also blue

like the cover of a file, like a nurse's skirt,

like a hospital gown, like a vein,

like the edge of a knife, like an old bruise,

like gravel in the jaws of the ebb and flow

like the colour that's between the death and life,

like the hard glass that's between us two.

NAN

We would count the days until she would arrive

– month

– fortnight

– day

the sands of time stretching like the Gobi in front of us

arrive whilst we were sleeping, she would

on the night bus from London in the morning.

Smelling her cigarettes

like gold, frankincense and myrrh on the landing

'Don't wake Nan – she's got jet-lag!'

We simmer outside her bedroom,

brimming with bubbles of excitement, like water

about to break the weir any minute,

gushing at her bedside

and drowning her in a hot whirlpool of arms.

Her case

full of treasures from Spain and Portugal –

little orange horses with velvet ears,

a school of chocolates in the shape of fish

are slippery drops between our fingers.

In the afternoon, at the far end of the garden,

Nan will be

painting hearts on my cheeks with lipstick,

Plaiting daisies into my hair,

dabbing drops of Tabu behind my two ears

('Don't tell your mum'),

I was pretty

despite being fat and wearing spectacles.

Nan scoring goals against Tomos

even though he was Spurs and she was Cwmtwrch Athletic.

Lying on her back in the grass afterwards,

laughing like golden syrup

and her eyes far away

on other horizons.

SLIPPING BY

There's a clean smell on the young German
leaning across the table, a smell of forests
and snow glistening in the sun
like dainty pieces of glass that have been shattered,

and the city
slips past on the U-bahn
the smooth wheels someone's oiled
and we know
that everything is going to happen just as it's meant to,

and by the light of the candle, we're talking about war
and look to the magic glass ball
to see people who live over the snow,
making pictures of the Gulf on the tablecloth
and using napkins
to mark out positions of tanks
and by the light of the candle, the night slips by
swiftly, like a child who's newly found
that he can skate

In the town today

I saw a man

pulling glass from a pipe

he was sucking all the air

and turning it all into a dream.

And on the naked branches, his glass balls hang

their colours purple and gold,

there's some secret to their making

that's too expensive for me to buy

that's too brittle for me to carry home to Wales.

And we're slipping past by candlelight

and the rails are so, so straight

slipping by on wheels someone's oiled

slipping by forever and ever and ever…

SWEEPING

For some strange reason

there isn't anywhere to leave your bags in Belfast central station.

So, while waiting for the train

on a Sunday afternoon, ecumenical in its boredom,

there was a need to minister against bomb preparations

ward over it devotionally

– in case its contents risk exploding

scattering ten pairs of black tights

to wave in a catholic way

over the ceremonial roofs of

the denominational city.

And as the rain started dropping

soft bullets of water

to fire a dance

on the tin roof,

I noticed that I had company

– a young man, in black clothes,

at it, sweeping Saturday night rubbish from the floor.

I watched him, I began to believe

that threatening filth,

banishing disorder,

was the burden of the quick movements;

came to understand

that the jerky stabbings of the brush

were more than what was technically required

to clear other people's mess.

And when the train came,

two hours later,

and the floor, for some while, had been cleaner than a nun's nightshirt,

he was still at it, sweeping

imaginary dust under an imaginary carpet.

BEFORE THE NEXT WAVE
a dolphin in Cardigan bay

Seeking the bay with tired eyes, and seeing

Epiphany in the middle of the summer in Aberystwyth

– Epiphany, night of odd offerings

and sparkling afternoon like a child's wrapping paper –

Dylan Eildon, baby of the sun and salt water

laughing in your crib, your green bed;

no mum but the waves to soothe your tears.

We, the imprudent ones, approach

to place our tributes at your breast –

faith, hope, love and vicissitude

for a moment of harmlessness before the wave,

before the next wave.

SOUP

This isn't a poem about soup -

not a poem about its aroma, its taste, nor its colour,

nor the stars of fat and its hot kisses

on the tongue that quickens their itch.

This isn't a poem about soup –

about a bite of tender carrot,

about the suck of a salty savoury sucking,

nor the parsley confetti of crinkled green.

Only soup it was, all told;

– potatoes and salt and meat and water –

not gazpacho nor chowder nor bouillabaisse

bisque nor velouté nor vichyssoise.

this isn't a poem about soup

but a poem about something that was half learned –

a pinch of something here and there,

a little more or a little less of the other

– the proper dish, a wooden spoon that's long enough

each boiling a new opportunity

to conjure the secret genius of soup.

This isn't a poem about soup at all –

not a poem about soup, nor about a scarcity of soup:

nothing to do with light and heat,

the radio's singing in a warm kitchen,

and space at the table.

USEFUL

I wonder what happened to the old women of my childhood?
their fur hats, their hymn books poised,
their love a hot pressure
of coarse material and spiky brooches?

I would writhe and slip from their grasp,
and the kiss of the brooch a bruise on my cheek.
behind the fuss and dead animals
the smell of sadness and sour wee.

'Love is love', rebuked my mum,
'whatever its smell might be,
despite its spikiness'.

Thus, I went,
and received love –
comforting love, sometimes,
slack and warm like old corduroy;
other love like net curtains
that reveal more than they hide;
one love like the bite of a rope
that strokes but burns my flesh.

This is the love I love;

love that's like sheets

of Irish linen, one hundred percent,

its texture smooth and strong

without a smell on it except cleanliness and powder;

sheets enough to hold the strong core

sheets that won't yield

when I knot them to themselves into a long white rope,

and hurl them from the window, to escape into the night.

POLITICAL CARTOONIST

Everything started as an abstraction,

a line cleaving acres from white paper

and the unyielding blackness revealing:

"Over there's there, here's here".

The line turned into a circle. In its linear order,

he inspected the space

between 'there' and 'here',

'inside', 'outside',

and 'black' and 'white'

– and all this,

the sense of the philosopher

not belonging to this world.

A circular face emerged – cheeks, and a nose

stranger than familiar.

Abstraction turned concrete,

judgement becomes part of the pattern.

They were caught.

The wet clay of the potter,

shavings of the carpenter,

the contention of the cartoonist – creating isn't

a nice and neat thing. It is words

more dissolute than soil, lines that are

weaker than wood. They were shot.

UTTERANCES

The eye of the well

the early flow,

the wild words rushing forward,

the parable of the water

between stony lumps in the river,

the sound of nonchalant sheep

gnawing the pasture;

and then at that the rustling between the branches of the trees,

green and white fingers

searching the meanings of afternoon summer,

pebbles in the torrent, patterning

that makes it possible – maybe –

to step to the other side

of the riverlike language

sweeping you forward towards something more –

the black limitless night, the salt becoming

a crust on your lip.

HANDIWORK

The smell of diesel in the car park
bruises the night. The sound of cigarettes sparks
a tattoo onto the darkness. I would like
for it to rain
if I were to be able to smoke;

eleven o clock, and tonight
there are men in masks wearing latex gloves,
proving their knife and sword blades,

starting on their perverse rites
in their blue gowns
under the white lights.

Tonight they will reveal the heart of his father,
strained with their blades
peeling back
in a web of filaments -

a cradle
for the smallest of nuts
that was ever to be seen.

BETWEEN TWO LIGHTS

Come for a walk to the dark parlour,

I've sailed the board towards tea;

the red berries and the china

are ready in their place.

We will have a feast of bread and home-made butter,

damson jam in a delicate dish,

and in the stuffy room where our table is

the clock marches on.

The knick-knacks on the mantlepiece wait,

the day-end winds slowly along the dingle,

and the sun casts shadows of the cups

across the white tablecloth.

Come to the table, my beautiful boy

– the place is full of cheese and shortcake.

But will you see… the two little birds, who are only bones, bones

above our crumbs?

WILLOW PATTERN, 1979

The everlasting afternoon
sinks into the crater of eventide,

as we wait its conclusion at Nain's house.

In the no-man's-land between hope and hopelessness,
'Pisyn, Pisyn' plays on the kitchen radio,

and we the family are bound in one breath,
not looking at the telly
nor through the wattle-work of fingers -

instead nailing our attention onto the dresser
tottering under its burden of dishware,
so strange and yet so familiar:

for us, the Welsh, it is not so black and white
– not so crude as that –
as the two who flee across the bridge,
the angry man and his crooked club on their tails
almost on the edge of catching them,
– the trees and their incredible shape

whispering

escape, maybe, is on the horizon –

the story, every time, in two halves.

COWBOYS

After his wife was dead,
he sat in the living room
with his back to the dresser.

The light fading,
as the sun set,
(no use sparking up the electric)
the night drawn in
like a coverlet over him.

There's enough light
from the small screen.
Shadows of men -
sometimes in black and white;
sometimes,
in Kodak SP
ensuring every cowboy's face
looks just like a tangerine.

Everlasting High Noon
at night, it was.

And as he sleeps

the noon train arrives,

and the man in the black shirt turns,

turns,

turns,

to face him, in the dust.

CONSERVING

To begin, set down your belongings. Remove

your everyday spectacles, take off your wedding ring

if you're wearing one. Put your watch to one side.

Before beginning, remember to clean your hands with the napkin

of designated paper, paying detailed attention

to the cuticles of your nails, and your fingers, the palm of your hand.

Finally, you may begin. Feel the cotton ball,

before clearing the paint, quietly and delicately.

no sound but for the dab, dab -

utterly patient, between the brown and the green

before reaching the impasto towards the bottom.

And here you are, coming to the least easy thing,

as your trip through the rainbow reaches completion, reaches white.

But there's something worse than this:

The colourless canvas, naked; waiting

for your attention. It is its turn to see the light of day.

CANOPY

And the rain is spitting, here on the beach:

Mum unfurls the umbrella

unrolls the clear plastic folds

of the hood of the buggy;

and as she straightens it,

she plays a game with her small son.

her hand touching his breath on the canopy,

her hand a starfish, answering back.

The rain snatches away her breath –

and her love's stark-naked jellyfish nearly suffocates her -

this transparent feeling

that demands its cleansing here and there, on the ebb

without anchor or landing-place.

A COPPICE IN MIDDELHARNIS
on thinking about Meidert Hobbema's painting

The church on the hill with its pepper-pot tower,

a handful of wild birds on the wind's bouncy castle

the girl in a white cap keeping up boring conversation

with a husband in a red-frock-coat and bandolier;

the tall rows of trees, like broccoli on legs

a mirror to the masts above the dyke and its rumour of escape.

This is her favourite picture. While the iron pig

procures pleats into the white shirts

her blunt knife scraping the pastry spares

from the bottom of the obstinate tin,

she's walking through the scenery, past the labyrinth

of dense leaves the colour of chocolate, black

the far edge to the whole perfect orchard,

Along the furrows where the mud and the mire

grasps at her heels, and she stumbles

towards the shadows that are at the far end of the path,

the hunter with his gun who's coming to meet her,

the nothing that's happening

over and over again.

SEARCHING

Feeling little, like an ant.

Going out to the trees

to see if you're there.

There's traces of your being here

the fire's embers

still smoulder.

The birds sup

on the loaf's crumbs,

the dirty plate;

I mountaineer across these enormous things.

Unable to see anything

beyond the bowl ocean.

No means of saying

whether the twigs on the floor

point at somewhere particular.

I would be searching for you after

between the old shopping trolleys

in the carparks where the rain

drives faster than the cars

in the tunnels that lead under the roads

towards the parks where the swings

hang crookedly, with a lump of dog poo

[how?] on the see-saw.

Sometimes, I think I see you

in the odd leaf

on the odd tree

that's throwing its arms to the sky

the

odd

pool of water

that reflects

something that the clouds are doing.

DEVELOPMENTS

'I don't want to lose you', he said

and set off for Thrace. Therefore

in order to be able to find me again

he left me

in a safe place,

sitting on a stone

on the shore.

He placed a camera in my

                        hands

and said to me

to film him, and the boys

                        leaving land.

Every morning we wake from a strange world

to a new land. Despite the sounds

of home, we rise from the new

to pursue duties.

The foam washed

the bottom of my frock,

and by the time his ship was nothing but

                      a comma

                      in the distance,

the sea had reached

                      up to my neck

and the film had soaked through.

***

I have grown a scab

like an old boat that's been

in the harbour too long.

My shoulders are heavy

                    beneath seaweed

and the beams are bowing

with the effort of me trying to remember your name.

            Oh yes.

I had something to say to you –

Do you see this spider's web that's

                    growing between my legs?

Look! And the moss

embroidering my pubis. Look!

and the goldfish who plays hide-and-seek

through the emptiness of my skull.

Look at me, won't you?

Look at me.

Love me.

After all, you made me.

SATING

If your memory, my love, is like some veil

of immeasurable water, without west, south

north, nor east either; without a face

but rather one edge the depth, and the other, the sky –

you can regret all the curelessness,

the unnecessary satire, the aphorisms

swift, unthinking; see them turning mute

and falling into the black perdition of the waves.

But by straitened memory, and the tide

wanting to hurl the wreckage of the past

on the sandbank of our today, this ocean won't do anything

but swallow the pain of the now in order to disgorge it tomorrow.

I will leave the boat of my shame to its wretchedness

sink it into nothing, the depth of your mercy.

ACKNOWLEDGEMENTS

This collection is a translation of *Dal i Fod* by Elin ap Hywel, published by Cyhoeddiadau Barddas. 'Developments' and 'The Poem's a Gauloise' first appeared in *Modern Poetry in Translation*. 'Before the Next Wave' first appeared in *Modron Magazine*.

My sincere thanks to Menna Elfyn for her warm support and encouragement from the very beginning of this project. And to Aaron Kent for responding to my submission of a pamphlet of Elin ap Hywel's poems by suggesting we do a full collection.

Deepest thanks to Ilmar Lehtpere, guide and mentor. Without him, neither this book nor any of my translations would exist.

LAY OUT YOUR UNREST

www.ingramcontent.com/pod-product-compliance
Lightning Source LLC
Chambersburg PA
CBHW032235080426
42735CB00008B/871